Save the Date

Carlos & Kat

WITHDRAWN

make it in
Minutes

Wedding Crafts

make it in
Minutes

Wedding Crafts

CATHERINE RISLING

LARK BOOKS

A Division of Sterling Publishing Co., Inc.
New York / London

Copy Editors
Lisa Anderson
Lecia Monsen

Photographer
Zachary Williams
Williams Visual

Stylist
Brittany Aardema

Book Designer
Kehoe+Kehoe Design
Associates

*Other Books
in This Series:*

Make It in Minutes:
Greeting Cards

Make It in Minutes:
Mini-Books

Make It in Minutes:
Mini-Boxes

Make It in Minutes:
Beaded Jewelry

Make It in Minutes:
Party Favors &
Hostess Gifts

Make It in Minutes:
Felt Accessories

Make It in Minutes:
Faux Floral Arrangements

Make It in Minutes:
Quick & Clever
Gift Wraps

Make It in Minutes:
Memory Jewelry

A Red Lips 4 Courage Communications, Inc., book
www.redlips4courage.com
Eileen Cannon Paulin
President

Catherine Risling
Director of Editorial

Library of Congress Cataloging-in-Publication Data
Risling, Catherine Yarnovich.
    Make It in minutes. Wedding crafts / by Catherine Risling.
    1st ed. p. cm.
    Includes index.
ISBN-13: 978-1-60059-228-7 (hc-plc with jacket : alk. paper)
ISBN-10: 1-60059-228-7 (hc-plc with jacket : alk. paper)
1. Handicraft. 2. Wedding Decorations. I. Title.
TT149.R54 2008
745.5--dc22

2007033283

10 9 8 7 6 5 4 3 2 1
First Edition

Published by Lark Books, A Division of
Sterling Publishing Co., Inc.
387 Park Avenue South, New York, N.Y. 10016

Text © 2008, Catherine Risling
Photography © 2008, Red Lips 4 Courage Communications, Inc.
Illustrations © 2008, Red Lips 4 Courage Communications, Inc.

Distributed in Canada by Sterling Publishing,
c/o Canadian Manda Group, 165 Dufferin Street
Toronto, Ontario, Canada M6K 3H6

Distributed in the United Kingdom by GMC Distribution Services,
Castle Place, 166 High Street, Lewes, East Sussex, England BN7 1XU

Distributed in Australia by Capricorn Link (Australia) Pty Ltd.,
P.O. Box 704, Windsor, NSW 2756 Australia

If you have questions or comments about this book, please contact:
Lark Books
67 Broadway
Asheville, NC 28801
(828) 253-0467

Manufactured in China

ISBN 13: 978-1-60059-228-7
ISBN 10: 1-60059-228-7

For information about custom editions, special sales, premium and corporate purchases, please contact Sterling Special Sales Department at (800) 805-5489 or specialsales@sterlingpub.com.

"Love is shown in your deeds,
not in your words."
—Fr. Jerome Cummings

Contents

Introduction

There are few things in life as exciting as getting married. Whether celebrations are held on a beach, at a restaurant, or in your best friend's backyard, the energy and excitement of the special day—spent with friends and family close to your heart—is a once-in-a-lifetime occasion.

When I married, I remember my mother telling me to walk slowly down the aisle and look at as many guests as possible; take it all in and enjoy it. That I did. I also took pleasure in all of the handcrafted touches—from photo displays featuring our guests at their own weddings to personal thank you notes that doubled as place cards. Few details went unnoticed and unappreciated.

Throughout this book you'll find dozens of fun ideas to personalize a wedding. You'll also find endearing gestures sure to impress your guests before, during, and after your celebration.

So whether you're getting married, or lending the bride a hand, I invite you to turn the page and discover the many ways you can create your own personal wedding touches.

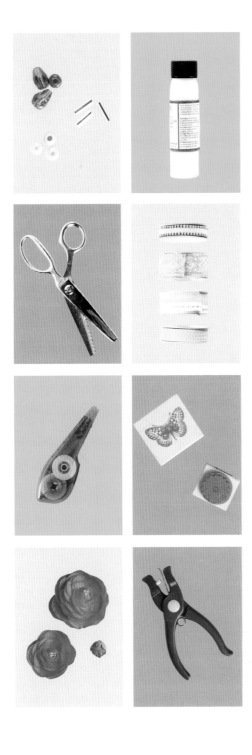

CHAPTER 1

Today there are so many wonderful embellishments readily available to help personalize wedding decorations, favors, invitations, and more. Choose charms that dangle, or glitter that adds the right amount of sophistication. Paper provides the base for most projects—from cardstock used to make invitations to poster board wrapped into a cone shape to boxes that can hold candy or a special message. Decorative paper allows you to personalize any of the projects in this book.

Choose your own colors or alter some of the details to fit your theme. Rather than flowers, for example, consider seashells or birds. Before you begin, be sure to review the materials, tools, and techniques you'll need to hand craft any of these unique projects in less than an hour.

Supplies

Armature wire
A modern choice in crafting today, armature wire is available in aluminum and copper. While it appears heavy duty, the lightweight and pliable wire is actually very easy to form simply using your fingers. Available in 4- to 16-gauge.

Beads
Beads add a decorative flair to any project. The smaller variety—seed and bugle—work best as accents, while larger beads can be tied to the ends of ribbon or layered to create the perfect finishing touch to a project. Beads can be adhered with craft or hot glue, eye pins, or double-sided tape, or strung on embroidery floss or ribbon.

Bird's nest
Readily available at craft stores, faux birds' nests are made in various sizes. Can be used as a centerpiece, place card holder, or wedding favor. Add oval or round candies in blue such as Jordan almonds to mimic eggs.

Boxes
Available in wood, papier-mâché, and cardboard. Boxes can be found in numerous sizes and shapes including rectangles, squares, ovals, and hearts. Boxes are ideal containers for wedding favors.

Brads
Available in a wide variety of colors, shapes, and sizes. Brads can be purely decorative or can be used to secure elements such as ribbon or paper. Some even have loops for stringing through ribbon or fibers, similar to lacing a shoe. To adhere, simply poke a small hole in the paper, insert the brad, and open the prongs on the back to secure.

Buttons
Buttons can make the perfect finishing touch to handmade projects. Sew or glue buttons with craft or hot glue to adhere.

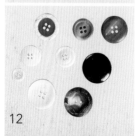

Candles
Few items bring warmth to a setting like candles. Available in jars and as votives, pillars, and tapers, candles make ideal favors and table decorations.

Candy
Who doesn't love a sweet treat? From mints to truffles, candy makes the perfect filler for decorated boxes, bottles, and cellophane bags that serve as wedding favors.

Cardstock
Cardstock provides a sturdy base for just about any project in this book. Can also be covered with decorative paper or fabric.

Charms
Charms are available in a variety of themes. Made from metal or plastic, charms can be glued or sewn to projects or dangled from ribbons or embroidery floss.

Decorative paper
Decorative and scrapbook paper is available in a wide variety of colors, types, weights, and textures. Can be adhered using practically any type of adhesive. For even coverage of larger sheets of paper, consider using an adhesive application machine. When using vellum, vellum adhesive tape works best.

Embroidery floss
Available in an array of colors, embroidery floss is a simple alternative to ribbon. Can be used to tie a project closed, hang charms from, or to provide a subtle accent.

time-saving tip

Make it Your Own
Cardstock makes a sturdy base for many craft projects. If you can't find the pattern or hue you are looking for, simply adhere desired decorative paper to a sheet of cardstock using an adhesive application machine.

Fabric
A wonderful element to dress up just about any project, fabric can be used in place of decorative or scrapbook paper to achieve the hue or theme you desire. Adhere with craft or fabric glue.

Felt
Readily available at craft stores, felt comes in a variety of colors, textures, and weights. Can be used to add shape, strength, and stiffness to projects. A handy option, adhesive-backed craft felt comes in a variety of colors.

Glitter—glass
Glass glitter is available in rich colors and sized from very fine to coarse. Glass glitter is not translucent and will completely cover the surface to which it is applied. Use with caution; it is glass and can cut the skin.

Glitter—glitter glue
Is it glitter, or is it adhesive—actually it's both! Packaged in small bottles, glitter glue is ideal for precise application and also for writing words or names.

Glitter—mica flakes
Though technically not a glitter, mica brings an antique, snow-like feel to projects.

Glitter—ultra-fine
Ultra-fine glitters are available in an amazing array of colors. Texture is similar to loose powder makeup, and a little goes a very long way.

Around the House

- Binder clips
- Computer and printer
- Copier
- Cotton balls
- Fine-tip black marker
- Paper towels
- Pencils
- Toothpicks
- Twine
- Waxed paper

Metal slide
Available in assorted shapes, metal slides are used for all sorts of projects, from jewelry making to key rings. Can also use glass pieces that are bound with metallic tape, adhesive, or stickers. Materials can be found in most craft stores.

Paint
Acrylic paint is the best way to color coordinate the surface of just about anything, from a wooden box to a papier-mâché letter or number. Apply paint with a foam or artist's brush. Spray paint can also be used, and is a quick alternative for all-over coverage.

Photographs
Photos of the bride and groom, guests, or the bride and/or groom with guests is one of the best ways to personalize a celebration. Survey your own stash of photos or borrow some from friends and family. Be sure to photocopy the image to preserve the original.

Pipe cleaners
These stems have a wire center and are covered with chenille. Can serve as a handle on a lightweight container, as an accent, or can be used to secure a project closed by tying around gathered paper or fabric. For a decorative finishing touch, twist the ends around a pencil to create spirals.

Polymer clay
This manmade clay is a wonderful way to create your own figures and shapes, like the Snowflake Clip in Chapter 3 used to hold a place card. Once it has been shaped, baked, and cooled, it can be painted and embellished.

Rhinestones
Rhinestones add an elegant sparkle to projects. Available in all sorts of colors, shapes, and sizes. Adhere to projects with craft glue.

15

Ribbon
Available in many widths and just about every hue, ribbon can be used to embellish nearly every project in this book. Consider using hand-dyed silks and fun ginghams.

Sealing wax
Traditionally used to secure letters and envelopes closed, sealing wax is a wonderful way to incorporate a monogram or simple design into a project. Available in the form of sticks, sometimes with a wick, or as granules.

Seashells
Seashells make wonderful accents. Use larger ones to fill a vase for a centerpiece or smaller shells to embellish an invitation or fashion into a unique name card.

Shredded paper
Available in a wide variety of colors, shredded paper adds a festive feel especially when it's spilling from a container.

Silk flowers
Made from ribbon or fabric, silk flowers create a lovely dimensional look. The same adhesives used with fabrics work well for silk flowers. Paper flowers, available in so many different sizes and colors, are a great alternative.

Wooden skewers
Readily available at most grocery stores, wooden skewers can be used to hold table numbers or photos. To trim, use heavy-duty craft scissors. Most come in 10" lengths.

time-saving tip
Filler Up
Shredded paper is available in many different hues, including some metallics. You may also want to consider using angel hair or other tinsel trims for an ethereal alternative.

Adhesives

Acid-free adhesive dispenser

Craft glue

Decoupage medium

Double-sided tape

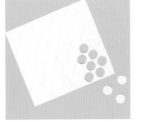

Foam mounting dots

Glitter adhesive

Glue stick

Hot-glue sticks

Peel-and-stick adhesive

Spray adhesive

Strong-hold glue

Vellum adhesive

Tools

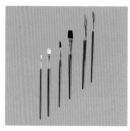

Artist's paintbrushes

Bone folder

Cosmetic sponges

Craft scissors

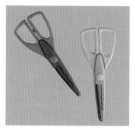

Decorative-edge scissors

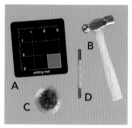

Eyelet-setting tools
A Setting mat   C Eyelets
B Craft hammer   D Eyelet setter

Floral snips

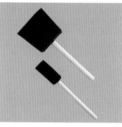

Foam brushes

Heat tool

Hole punch

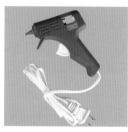

Hot-glue gun

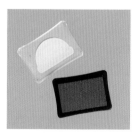

Inkpad

Needle-nose pliers

Paper punch

Paper trimmer

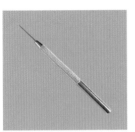

Piercing tool

Pinking shears

Rubber stamps

Ruler

Sandpaper

Scoring tool

Sealing wax stamps

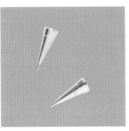

Ultra-fine metal tip

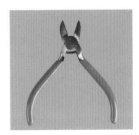

Wire cutters

Techniques

Adhering micro beads

These tiny no-hole beads are adhered much the same way as glitter. For projects such as the Picture Them Box in Chapter 4, use a sheet of peel-and-stick adhesive. Simply trace the surface of your project onto the sheet (Fig. 1), cut out (Fig. 2), lay adhesive onto surface of project (Fig. 3), peel backing off adhesive (Fig. 4), and then sprinkle micro beads to cover (Fig. 5). Be sure to firmly adhere any loose beads by pressing in place (Fig. 6).

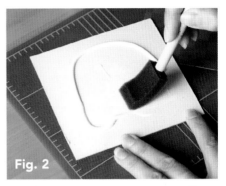

Fig. 1

Fig. 2

Fig. 3

Applying glitter

With slight pressure, glide tip of glitter adhesive or craft glue across paper or project surface to achieve the thinnest, smoothest, most intact line of adhesive possible. Add more pressure to make different line widths. Using a spoon, sprinkle glitter on glue then tap off excess (Fig. 1). It is important to apply the glitter to the glue while it is wet, white, and shiny, between 30–60 seconds. Glitter does not stick well to glue that has begun to dry. Use glitter adhesive in a squeeze bottle with a fine tip to outline images or add borders.

Covering chipboard and mitering corners

Apply a thin layer of craft glue to one side of the chipboard piece using a foam brush (Fig. 2). Place chipboard, glue side down, onto backside of decorative paper. Trim paper diagonally across all of the corners just outside of the chipboard piece. *Note:* The distance of the cut from the chipboard corners should be equal to the thickness of the chipboard. Fold and adhere paper onto the backside of the chipboard (Fig. 3).

Glittering Large Surfaces

time-saving tip

For wider coverage, brush the surface of your project with craft glue and immediately sprinkle on glitter. Glitter can also be mixed directly into your glue for sparkling coverage.

Fig. 1

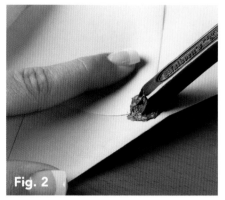

Fig. 2

Fig. 3

Fig. 4

Creating sealing wax seals

Hold stick of wax over a candle flame, but not too close as it will burn (Fig. 1). When the wax gradually softens, apply it with a circular movement on the place to be sealed (Fig. 2); rub it around and down until you have desired size and thickness. While the wax is still soft, impress a seal with a monogram or design (Fig. 3) and let dry (Fig. 4). To make a seal that will be attached later, drop melted wax on waxed paper and press with seal; let it dry, and then adhere seal to project surface with craft glue.

Distressing with ink

To age a tag, box, playing card, image, or paper, run the inkpad directly around the edges then smudge with a cosmetic sponge or your fingers. You can also randomly blot the surface to age the piece even more. Charcoal gray and brown are good inkpad colors to use.

time-saving tip

Creating Lasting Seals

Use real wax sticks that contain a little polymer for flexibility. This will ensure that the wax does not get too brittle and crack when mailing or being handled.

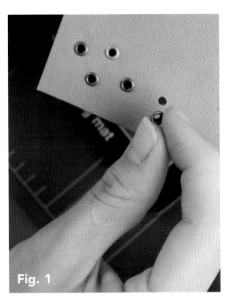

Fig. 1

Fig. 2

Fig. 3

Setting eyelets

To set eyelets in paper, punch a small hole where the eyelet is to be set (Fig. 1). Insert the eyelet through the hole and position the project face down on a craft mat. Using a setting tool and hammer, flatten the eyelet's backside to secure it in place (Fig. 2). *Note:* Some eyelet-setting systems vary; simply follow the manufacturer's instructions.

Rubber stamping

For the best effect, pat the stamp on the inkpad several times (Fig. 3). Press firmly onto the desired surface. Lift off carefully without smearing ink. *Note:* Permanent ink typically dries quickly while pigment ink may take some time. To speed drying time, set permanent ink with a heat tool.

Working with wire

Use needle-nose pliers to bend wire into desired shapes. Some pliers also double as wire cutters when the wire is pushed close to the hinge. Thin wire can be cut with craft scissors.

We're Getting Married...
In Hawaii!

Daniella Andrews
and
Andreas Nicholson

Please join us for a week
of love, laughter,
and memories
March 18-24

ISLAND

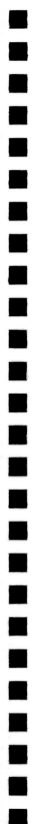

CHAPTER 2

Share your excitement for impending nuptials with a handmade save the date announcement or invitation. Tailor the look to just about any theme—from elegant to nautical to downright fun and festive.

A computer and printer come in handy to help set the tone with the right font—whether formal or funky. Print the details then create an envelope, super-size tag, or memorable map ensemble. Or, fashion a snow globe with a plastic half dome and felt backing. Inside are the details, along with glitter that resembles snow and a vintage-inspired image of a church.

All you need is cardstock for the base of any of these projects and some simple embellishments to create invitations that remind guests of the big day.

Save the Date Envelope

Materials

- Acid-free adhesive dispenser
- Bone folder
- Cardstock: coordinating patterns (2); white
- Computer and printer
- Decorative paper: coordinating
- Decorative-edge scissors
- Paper punch: 2" circle
- Paper trimmer
- Ruler

Instructions

1. **To make envelope:** Cut white cardstock to 10" x 7". Fold up bottom about 1½" to form base using bone folder. Fold in sides 4" using bone folder. Using adhesive dispenser, adhere back flaps together and adhere at bottom of envelope. Paper punch top center of envelope.

2. Cut decorative cardstock into two pieces, 2½" x 9" and 2" x 9", using decorative-edge scissors for one of the pieces and the paper trimmer for the other. Layer pieces and wrap around envelope, adhering with adhesive dispenser.

3. **To make invitation:** Cut 3½" x 5½" piece of coordinating cardstock. Using decorative-edge scissors, trim top and bottom. Print invitation details on decorative paper and then cut to 2½" x 4½"; trim all edges with decorative-edge scissors. Adhere decorative paper to front of cardstock using adhesive dispenser.

4. Insert invitation in envelope.

Photo Ornament

Materials

- Cardstock
- Computer and printer
- Craft scissors
- Decorative paper: old newsprint
- Floral image: small
- Glass slides: 1" x 3" (2)
- Glue stick
- Inkpad: charcoal gray
- Metal frame: 1" x 3"
- Pencil
- Ribbon
- Ruler
- Vintage wedding photo

Instructions

1. Cut cardstock to 1" x 3".

2. **To make side one:** Trace glass slide on decorative paper; cut out and adhere to cardstock. Cut vintage image to 1" x 2¼", centering focal point; adhere on top of decorative paper.

3. **To make side two:** Trace glass slide on decorative paper; cut out and adhere to cardstock. Using computer, print "Save the Date" details on cardstock; cut to 2" x ½". Gently wipe edge of cardstock on inkpad; let dry and then adhere to decorative paper at an angle. Trim floral image closely and then adhere to top right of decorative paper.

4. Sandwich decorative paper, which is now two-sided, between glass slides. Insert in metal frame and secure to close.

5. Tie 14" length of ribbon to top of ornament; trim ends at an angle.

time-saving tip

Simplify with the Right Cardstock

Save a few steps by using two-sided cardstock. This will allow you to coordinate patterns without having to cut and paste two sheets of decorative paper onto the cardstock.

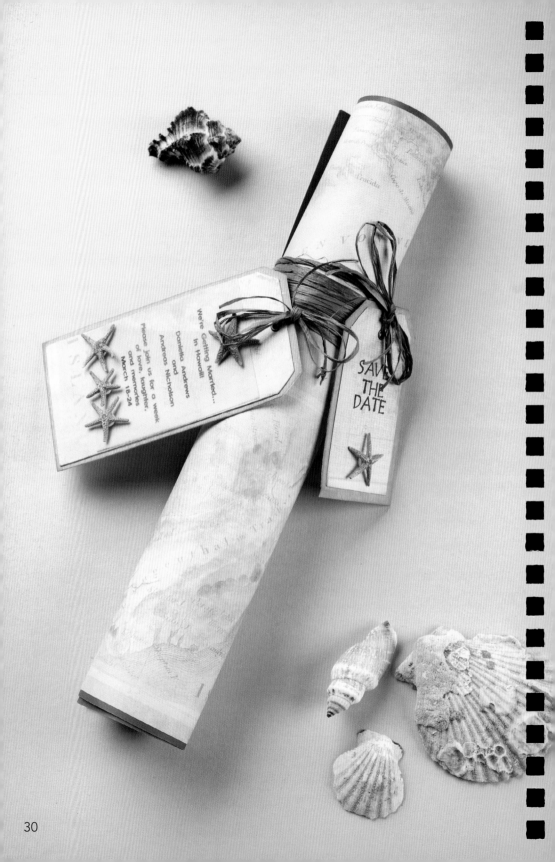

We're Getting Married...
in Hawaii!

Daniella Andrews
and
Andreas Nicholson

Please join us for a week
of love, laughter,
and memories
March 18-24

SAVE
THE
DATE

Map Announcement

Materials

- Adhesives: foam dots, glue stick, vellum tape
- Computer and printer
- Craft scissors
- Decorative paper: 12¼" x 12¼" dark brown, light brown
- Eyelet-setting tools
- Eyelets: small bronze (2)
- Inkpad: black
- Pencil
- Raffia: blue
- Rubber stamps: alphabet letters
- Scrapbook paper: 12" x 12" map (2)
- Shipping tags: medium, small (1 each)
- Starfish: mini (5)
- Vellum: light blue

Instructions

1. Center and adhere scrapbook paper to dark brown decorative paper with glue stick; set aside.

2. Trace tag shapes onto light brown decorative paper; cut out. Adhere to tags with glue stick.

3. Trace tags onto scrapbook paper; trim about ¼" smaller than tag shapes. Adhere to tags with glue stick.

4. Stamp "Save the Date" onto small tag. Set eyelet at top of tag. Add starfish using foam dot.

5. Print wedding details onto vellum. Cut to fit larger tag and adhere with vellum tape. Add starfish using foam dots.

6. Roll layered decorative and scrapbook papers; wrap with raffia. Slip tags onto raffia and then tie into bows.

the Date!

Kenneth
and
Debbie

Save the Date Tag

Materials

- Bone folder
- Brads: silver (8)
- Cardstock: two-sided; white
- Computer and printer
- Glue stick
- Hole punch
- Leafing pen: silver
- Pencil
- Piercing tool
- Ribbon
- Scissors: craft, decorative-edge
- Scrapbook flower: white
- Scrapbook frame

Instructions

1. **To make envelope:** Trace Envelope Template (page 34) onto two-sided cardstock; cut out. Trim each end with decorative-edge scissors. Score at line and fold in half. Score and fold top edge. Pierce four evenly spaced holes down each side, about $\frac{1}{4}$" in from edge; insert brads. Add scrapbook flower. Print couple's name on white cardstock; cut out and insert in scrapbook frame. Adhere to front of envelope.

2. **To make tag:** Trace Tag Template (page 34) onto white cardstock; cut out using decorative-edge scissors. Outline edges with leafing pen. Print details onto white cardstock; cut to $2\frac{1}{2}$" square. Outline edges with leafing pen and then adhere to front of tag with glue stick. Punch hole at top of tag and insert ribbon.

time-saving tip

Dress Them Up

To spruce up plain flower cutouts, simply color the edges of the petals with leafing pens, chalks, or inkpads and embellish the center with seed beads.

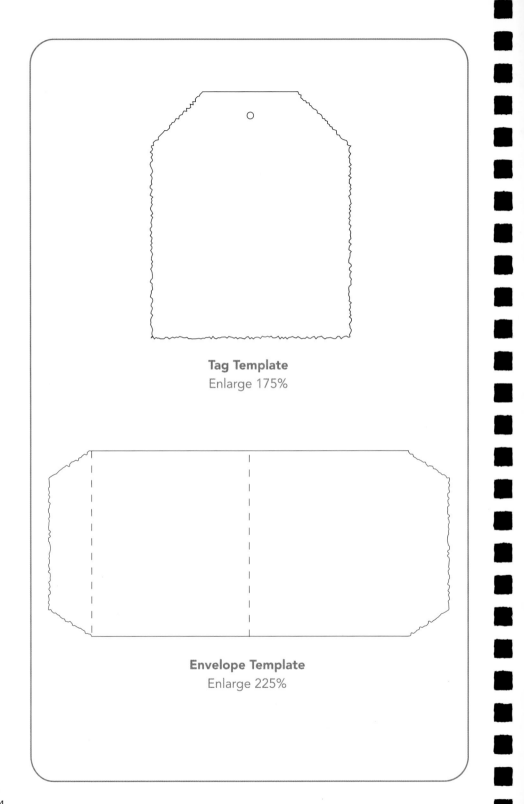

Tag Template
Enlarge 175%

Envelope Template
Enlarge 225%

Super-Size Tag

Materials

Instructions

1. Trace Tag Template (page 40) onto cardstock; cut out.

2. **To decorate front of card:** Using computer, print "Save the Date" details onto center bottom of tag. Cut coordinating decorative papers to 4"x 11½" and 2½"x 2". Cut photo to 2"x 1⅓". Layer and adhere with glue stick on front of tag, referring to project photo for placement.

3. **To decorate back of tag:** Cut coordinating decorative papers into following sizes: 4"x 4", 4"x 2½", 4"x 1½", 4"x 1¼", and ½"x 4". Layer on back of tag, referring to project photo on page 41 for placement. Add buttons with craft glue.

4. Punch hole at top of tag. Cut 14" length of ribbon and tie in hole; trim ends of ribbon at an angle.

time-saving tip

Copy in Quantity

To make several Super-Size tags quickly, consider photocopying the original. A good-quality copier will resemble the original image.

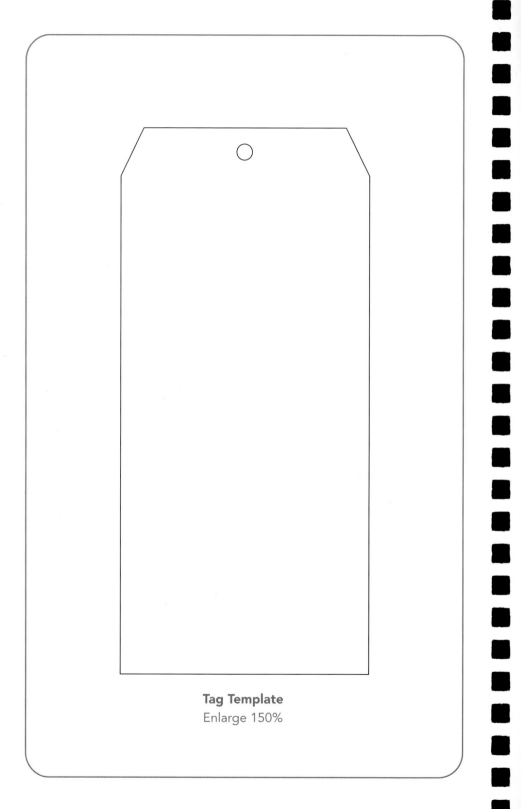

Tag Template
Enlarge 150%

Photo Magnet

Materials

- Adhesives: fabric glue, glue stick
- Beads: glass (1), seed (3)
- Binder clips
- Charm
- Computer, printer, scanner
- Craft scissors
- Craft wire
- Decorative paper
- Image
- Mint tin
- Pencil
- Photo-editing software
- Piercing tool
- Ribbon
- Self-adhesive magnet

Instructions

1. Separate mint tin; discard base. Trace lid onto decorative paper; cut out. Adhere to inside of lid with glue stick.

2. Cut ribbon to fit around mint tin. Apply fabric glue along inside and outside edges of tin; press ribbon onto glue to adhere in place. Hold with binder clips; set aside.

3. Using photo-editing software, scan image and then add desired sentiment. Crop to fit inside lid; print and then cut out. Adhere to inside of lid with glue stick.

4. Using piercing tool, make hole at bottom of tin. String beads on craft wire, looping charm at bottom. Insert wire through hole. Add seed bead inside tin and twist wire to hold in place.

5. Add adhesive-backed magnet to back of lid.

time-saving tip

Instant Image Ideas

If you don't have access to photo-editing software, simply cut your image to fit inside the lid and adhere with a glue stick. Then print sentiment on cardstock, cut to fit, and adhere on top of image with a glue stick. An old postcard, decorative paper, or copy of a photograph can be used as the focal point.

CHAPTER 3

Name cards are a wonderful way to set a theme, personalize a place setting, and even toss in a little fun.

Pinecones and snowflakes are perfect for winter, while birds and seashells lend more of a summer or springtime feel. Everyday playing cards and shipping tags are evergreen; you're only limited by your imagination.

To heighten the presentation, let your computer do the printing on cardstock that will serve as the place card or decorative paper that can be adhered to a firmer surface. Choose a pre-cut size or trim the edges with decorative-edge scissors. Then it's on to embellishing. Use your own drawing skills or rubber stamp an image. Photocopies of old wedding portraits can also be cut out and adhered for a vintage feel.

Playing Card

Materials

- Cosmetic sponge
- Craft scissors
- Decorative paper
- Glue stick
- Inkpad: light brown
- Letter stickers
- Pencil
- Playing card
- Sandpaper

Instructions

1. Trace playing card onto decorative paper; cut out. Adhere to backside of playing card with glue stick.

2. Lightly sand front and sides of playing card. Using cosmetic sponge, randomly apply ink to edges and both sides of playing card.

3. Add sticker letters spelling out guest's name to front of playing card.

time-saving tip

Choose Your Cards Wisely

Playing cards come in all sorts of patterns. A quick search on the Internet will turn up a wide variety. Consider the theme and colors; choose one that appeals to you and then you can skip adhering decorative paper to the backs of the cards.

Chipboard Bird

Materials

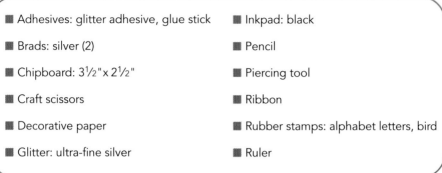

- Adhesives: glitter adhesive, glue stick
- Brads: silver (2)
- Chipboard: $3\frac{1}{2}$" x $2\frac{1}{2}$"
- Craft scissors
- Decorative paper
- Glitter: ultra-fine silver
- Inkpad: black
- Pencil
- Piercing tool
- Ribbon
- Rubber stamps: alphabet letters, bird
- Ruler

Instructions

1. Trace chipboard onto decorative paper twice; cut out. Adhere to front and back of chipboard with glue stick.

2. Cover edges of chipboard with glitter adhesive. Sprinkle on glitter; let dry.

3. Stamp bird image on front of chipboard; let dry.

4. Cut $3\frac{1}{2}$" length of ribbon. Stamp name in center. Mark and pierce holes on either side of chipboard about $\frac{1}{4}$" in. Adhere ribbon to chipboard with brads.

time-saving tip

Print, Don't Stamp

Rather than use ribbon and a rubber stamp, print your guest's name on cardstock using a computer. Simply cut out the name strip to fit the width of your chipboard and adhere using a glue stick.

Vintage Image

Materials

- Adhesives: dimensional, glue stick
- Cardstock: cream
- Computer and printer
- Cosmetic sponge
- Craft scissors
- Decorative paper
- Eyelet: silver square
- Eyelet-setting tools
- Inkpad: light brown
- Pencil
- Ribbon
- Scrapbook frame: self-adhesive silver
- Shipping tag
- Vintage image: wedding couple

Instructions

1. Trace shipping tag onto decorative paper twice; cut out. Adhere to front and back of tag with glue stick.

2. Cut out vintage image close to the figure. Cover image with dimensional adhesive; let dry completely. Adhere image to front of tag with glue stick.

3. Set eyelet at top of tag.

4. Using computer, print name on cardstock; cut out and then ink edges using cosmetic sponge. Adhere inside scrapbook frame and then add frame to front of tag.

5. Thread ribbon through eyelet at top of tag and knot.

54

Snowflake Clip

Materials

- 1" glass block
- Adhesives: craft glue, hot glue, spray adhesive
- Armature wire: silver
- Cardstock: cream
- Computer and printer
- Cookie cutter: 2" snowflake
- Craft scissors
- Miniature clothespin
- Pencil
- Polymer clay: transparent
- Rolling pin
- Ruler
- Spray paint: silver
- Ultra-fine glitter: multi-colored silver

Instructions

1. Roll out polymer clay. Cut shape using cookie cutter. Insert 14" piece of wire half way up shape. Bake shape according to manufacturer's instructions; let dry.

2. Spray shape with adhesive. Sprinkle on glitter to cover; let dry.

3. Spray paint miniature clothespin silver; let dry. Adhere to back of snowflake using craft glue; let set.

4. Twist ends of wire around pencil. Adhere to glass block using hot glue.

5. Using computer, print guest's name on cardstock. Cut out and insert in clip.

time-saving tip

Keep it Simple

Polymer clay comes in all sorts of colors. Keep the snowflake design simple by omitting the glitter.

Bird's Nest

Materials

- Angel hair: white
- Bird's nest: 4"
- Candy-coated almonds: blue
- Cardstock: cream
- Computer and printer
- Hot glue gun and glue sticks
- Ribbon: black-and-white gingham; pink rickrack; silver feather metallic
- Scissors: craft, decorative-edge

Instructions

1. Hot glue feather metallic ribbon around bird's nest. Layer gingham ribbon and pink rickrack, and then adhere on top of metallic ribbon with hot glue.

2. Fill nest with angel hair and then place almonds on nest.

3. Using computer, print guest's name on cardstock; trim with decorative-edge scissors. Insert name card in candy at an angle.

time-saving tip

Nesting Options

If you can't find white angel hair, consider using cotton balls, white shredded paper, or a layer of white felt to line the bird's nest.

William
&
Lisa

Starfish & Shell

Materials

- Craft glue
- Dried flowers
- Fine-tip marker: black
- Glass glitter: crystal
- Hot glue gun and glue sticks
- Rock
- Seashell
- Starfish

Instructions

1. Line outside of shell with craft glue; cover with glitter and let dry.

2. Position starfish on rock; hot glue in place.

3. Place shell in hand. Write guests' names in shell; hot glue onto rock. Adhere dried flowers using craft glue.

time-saving tip

Avoid the Frustration

If your seashell has imperfections that make it difficult to write on, you may want to print the guest's name (or names) on cardstock using a computer and then attach it to the shell with putty or double-sided tape for a temporary hold.

Pinecone

Materials

- Brads: antique gold (2)
- Cardstock: cream
- Computer and printer
- Craft scissors
- Piercing tool

- Pinecone
- Ribbon
- Ruler
- Spray adhesive
- Ultra-fine glitter: multi-colored gold

Instructions

1. Spray adhesive all over pinecone. Immediately sprinkle lightly with glitter; set aside to dry.

2. Cut ribbon about 1" shorter than circumference of pinecone; set aside.

3. Using computer, print guest's name on cardstock. Cut to $2\frac{1}{2}$" x $\frac{3}{4}$", trimming ends in inverted "V" shape.

4. Using piercing tool, poke holes about $\frac{1}{4}$" in from ends of cardstock. Wrap ribbon around pinecone. Insert brads through cardstock and then through ribbon.

time-saving tip

Making Cents

A quick way to stabilize a leaning pinecone is to hot glue a coin to the bottom surface.

Asian Flair

Materials

- Cardstock: cream
- Chopsticks
- Computer and printer
- Craft scissors
- Fine-tip marker: black
- Ruler
- Snap purse
- Watercolor pen: red

Instructions

1. To make place card: Using computer, print guest's name on cardstock. Cut to 3" x 2¼". Draw bamboo shoots with black marker; accent with red flowers using watercolor pen, referring to project photo for design.

2. Insert chopsticks in center of snap purse. Insert place card. *Note:* You may want to fill the snap purse with pebbles or sand to hold the chopsticks in place and to give weight to the project.

time-saving tip

Stamp it Up

Instead of hand drawing the floral design on the place card, use a rubber stamp. Craft stores stock all sorts of Asian-themed stamps that can be stamped in color, or stamped in black and accented with colored pencils, pens, or markers.

CHAPTER 4

Wedding favors have long been part of place settings to thank guests for joining the bride and groom. The key to a favorable favor is the presentation; with such pretty packaging, who can wait to see what's inside? And thanks to all of the wonderful embellishments on the market today, ideas are seemingly endless.

Vellum envelopes filled with lavender fill the air with fragrance, while beautifully adorned boxes that open to reveal truffles or other tasty treats make creative keepsakes.

With decorative paper and craft wire, create a pretty holder for a CD made in honor of the bride and groom. Be sure to use paper scraps and leftover ribbon to dress up the CD cover.

Don't forget monograms and photographs—both are great ways to personalize favors and the wedding celebration.

Lavender Envelope

Materials

- Adhesives: double-sided tape, foam squares, glitter adhesive
- Cardstock: white
- Craft scissors
- Dresden initial: gold
- Dried lavender
- Glitter: ultra-fine purple
- Mini hole punch
- Paper punches: 2" round, 2½" scallop-edged
- Printed tissue paper
- Ribbon
- Vellum envelope

Instructions

1. Fill envelope with dried lavender; seal closed.

2. Punch circle out of cardstock using scallop-edged paper punch. Using mini hole punch, punch holes around perimeter.

3. Punch 2" round circle out of printed tissue paper. Adhere to top of cardstock using double-sided tape.

4. Wrap ribbon around envelope, securing with double-sided tape. Add circles to front of envelope with foam squares.

5. Apply glitter adhesive to initial and sprinkle on glitter; let dry. Adhere to front of envelope with foam squares.

time-saving tip

Add More Fragrance

If you can't find the right size initial, simply replace the design element with small sprigs of lavender tied to the ribbon.

CD Holder

Materials

- Adhesives: glue stick, hot glue
- Armature wire: silver
- Bone folder
- Buttons: different sizes (2)
- Cardstock: 12"-square double-sided
- CD case
- Eyelet-setting tools
- Eyelets: silver (2)
- Mini hole punch
- Paper flowers, leaves
- Pencil
- Ribbon
- Ruler
- Scissors: craft, pinking shears
- Wire cutters

Instructions

1. Using pencil, trace CD Holder Template (page 70) onto cardstock; cut out with craft scissors. Trim right and left sides using pinking shears. Fold on fold lines using bone folder.

2. Referring to template, punch two holes on backside of cardstock. Insert eyelet in each hole and secure using eyelet-setting tools.

3. Cut two 12" lengths of armature wire. Insert through eyelets and secure at back by twisting ends together.

time-saving tip

Embellish with the Leftovers

Use leftover cardstock to fashion a matching label for the CD tin, which is inserted into the holder.

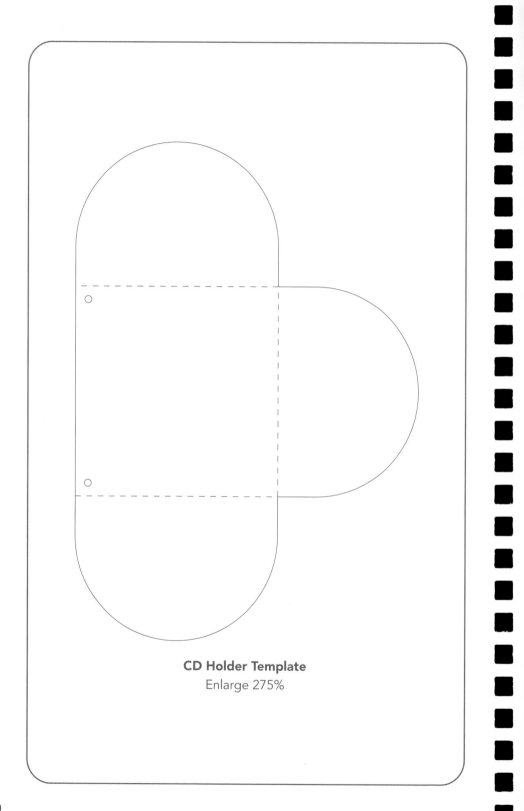

CD Holder Template
Enlarge 275%

Above: Leftover embellishments and decorative paper are ideal for adorning the front of the CD case.

4. Layer buttons and paper flower, hot gluing to secure. Attach to front of CD holder with two layers of hot glue, letting first layer dry completely before adding second layer. *Note:* This will provide space to insert paper leaves.

5. Cut 24" length of ribbon. Hot glue at center of back of holder. Wrap around CD holder, securing in place with glue stick. Insert paper leaves, securing in place with glue stick. Decorate CD case as desired and then insert in CD holder.

time-saving tip

Two-Sided Solution

If you can't find double-sided cardstock in the right colors, simply adhere two one-sided pieces together using an adhesive application machine.

Floral Heart Box

Materials

- Acrylic paint: cream
- Adhesives: craft glue, double-sided tape, glitter adhesive, hot glue
- Beaded wire
- Craft scissors
- Foam brush

- Glass glitter: crystal
- Paper flower buds: small
- Rhinestones: rectangular
- Ribbon
- Silk flowers, leaves
- Wooden box: 4" heart

Instructions

1. Paint box cream; let dry.

2. Cover sides with glitter adhesive. Sprinkle on glass glitter; let dry completely.

3. On rim around top of box, adhere ribbon using double-sided tape. Embellish ribbon with rhinestones, adhering with craft glue.

4. Make several loops with 2" pieces of ribbon. Adhere ends together with craft glue; set aside to dry.

5. Adhere silk flowers and leaves to top of box using hot glue. Tuck ribbon loops under flowers using hot glue.

6. Wrap paper flower buds with beaded wire. Adhere buds randomly in between silk flowers using hot glue.

time-saving tip

Look out for Ready-Made

To save time, purchase small beaded flowers rather than creating your own. Also, many craft stores carry self-adhesive rhinestones so be on the lookout!

Picture Them Box

Materials

- Adhesives: craft glue, glue stick, peel-and-stick sheet
- Cardstock: ivory
- Computer and printer
- Cosmetic sponge
- Craft knife
- Craft scissors
- Decorative paper
- Inkpads: dark brown, light brown
- Micro beads: clear
- Pencil
- Photo of couple
- Ribbon
- Rubber stamps: alphabet
- Ruler
- Scrapbook frame: self-adhesive silver
- Wooden box

Instructions

1. **To decorate lid:** Trace top and sides of box lid on decorative paper; cut out and adhere with glue stick. Using craft knife, cut out 3" x 4" piece of decorative paper in center of lid. Cut photo to this size and adhere inside space with glue stick. Trace top of lid onto peel-and-stick adhesive; cut out and add to lid top. Peel off backing and sprinkle micro beads to cover; press in place. Ink edges of box with light brown ink and cosmetic sponge. Stamp desired sentiment around lid with dark brown ink.

2. **To decorate base:** Trace sides of box on decorative paper; cut out and adhere with glue stick. Wrap ribbon around box, securing in place with glue stick. Using computer, print name of bride and groom on cardstock. Ink edges and cut to fit inside metal frame, and then adhere with craft glue. Adhere frame to front of box.

3. Fill with shredded paper and treats, if desired.

Bucket of Good Wishes

Materials

- Adhesives: craft glue, hot glue
- Cardstock: cream
- Decorative paper
- Foam core
- Glittered star
- Mini hole punch
- Netting: black
- Paper trimmer
- Pipe cleaner: silver
- Rhinestones
- Ruler
- Scissors: craft, decorative-edge
- Shredded paper
- Treats

Instructions

1. Cut 3" circle out of foam core.

2. Cut decorative paper to fit around foam core using paper trimmer; trim top with decorative-edge scissors. Adhere around foam core base with craft glue, overlapping edges.

3. Cut 3¼"x ½" piece of cardstock. Trim one side with decorative-edge scissors. Adhere rhinestones with craft glue every ¾"; let set. Wrap cardstock around base, overlapping edges and securing with craft glue.

4. Layer netting and glittered star on front of "bucket," adhering with hot glue.

5. Punch holes on opposite sides of bucket. Insert pipe cleaner, looping ends to secure in place.

6. Insert shredded paper and desired treats.

time-saving tip
Household Helper

To create a perfect circle, trace the opening of a drinking glass onto your cardstock and cut out.

Sweet Treats

Materials

- Adhesives: double-sided tape, hot glue, strong-hold glue
- Beaded pin
- Beads: assorted
- Button
- Candy
- Glass jar with cork
- Ribbon: coordinating (2)

Instructions

1. Fill jar with candy.

2. Layer and adhere ribbon around bottom base of jar using double-sided tape. Adhere coordinating ribbon around top of jar.

3. Adhere button to top of cork with hot glue. *Note:* If cork size overpowers the jar, trim with serrated knife.

4. Layer beads on pin; insert pin through button into cork, securing in place with strong-hold glue.

time-saving tip

Serving Double Duty

The Sweet Treats wedding favor can also double as a place card. Simply write the guest's name on cardstock, hole punch, and then thread onto ribbon and tie ribbon around the jar.

Tea Tin

Materials

- Adhesives: craft glue, foam squares
- Cardstock: textured (2)
- Computer and printer
- Craft scissors
- Rhinestones
- Ribbon
- Ruler
- Silver tin
- Toothpick

Instructions

1. Using computer, print monogram of bride and groom on cardstock. Cut to 2" square.

2. Using toothpick, add dot of craft glue to backside of rhinestones; adhere around perimeter of monogram square.

3. Tie ribbon in bow around tin. Glue monogram to 2½" square of coordinating cardstock and then adhere to front of tin with foam squares.

Dazzling Dots
time-saving tip

Glitter glue is a sparkling yet simple alternative to rhinestones. Simply squeeze out small dots around the monogram and let dry completely.

Wrapped Candles

Materials

- Beads: coordinating (3)
- Craft scissors
- Decorative paper: coordinating (2)
- Double-sided tape
- Embroidery floss: cream
- Ribbon
- Ruler
- Silk flowers
- Taper candles: 4

Instructions

1. Cut decorative paper to 9" x 4½" and 9" x 4". Layer and adhere together with double-sided tape to create band.

2. Wrap band around candles, adhering at back with double-sided tape. Tie ribbon into bow around band. String 1½" of beads on two pieces embroidery floss. Trim floss to 3" and then tie knots at top and bottom to keep beads in place.

3. Insert silk flowers and tie to beads to embellish.

time-saving tip

Paper Dominates & Decorates

Layered decorative papers make beautiful accents on their own. To save time, keep it simple and tie embroidery floss around the band without adding beads.

CHAPTER 5

Details, details—and boy, do we have some good ones. Make projects from scratch, like the sign-in booklet or table number, or embellish store-bought items such as the beaded pen. Glitter, beads, and scrapbooking embellishments are quick and easy ways to spruce things up.

Use fabric and layered ribbons to decorate a photo box, creating a pretty receptacle for cards, or add paint and Swarovski crystals to dress up toasting glasses and a cake knife.

Gather wedding photos of your guests (this will have to be started months before the wedding day) and make photocopies to use in photo stands placed on each table. Your guests will have so much fun comparing hairstyles and wedding dresses, and sharing memories of their own special day.

Table Number

Materials

- Acrylic paint: cream
- Adhesives: craft glue, glue stick, hot glue, spray adhesive
- Craft scissors
- Decorative paper
- Floral foam
- Foam brush
- Mica
- Paper punch: 2½" decorative-edge circle
- Papier-mâché box: 3" circle
- Pearl embellishments, trim
- Piercing tool
- Ruler
- Spray paint: silver
- Wooden number
- Wooden skewer

Instructions

1. Spray paint number and wooden skewer silver; let dry.

2. Spray number with spray adhesive and cover with mica.

3. Paint papier-mâché box cream; let dry. Insert 2" square of floral foam inside box, securing in place with hot glue.

4. Measure and cut decorative paper to fit around bottom of box; adhere with glue stick. Create circle out of decorative paper using paper punch; adhere to top of box with glue stick.

5. Add pearl trim to top and bottom of box, securing in place with craft glue.

6. Pierce hole at center of top of lid. Wrap pearl trim around skewer, securing in place with hot glue. Insert skewer in top of box. Add pearl embellishments on top of lid and under number.

time-saving tip

Two in One

Save time by combining your centerpiece and the table number. Simply stick the skewer in a potted plant or floral arrangement.

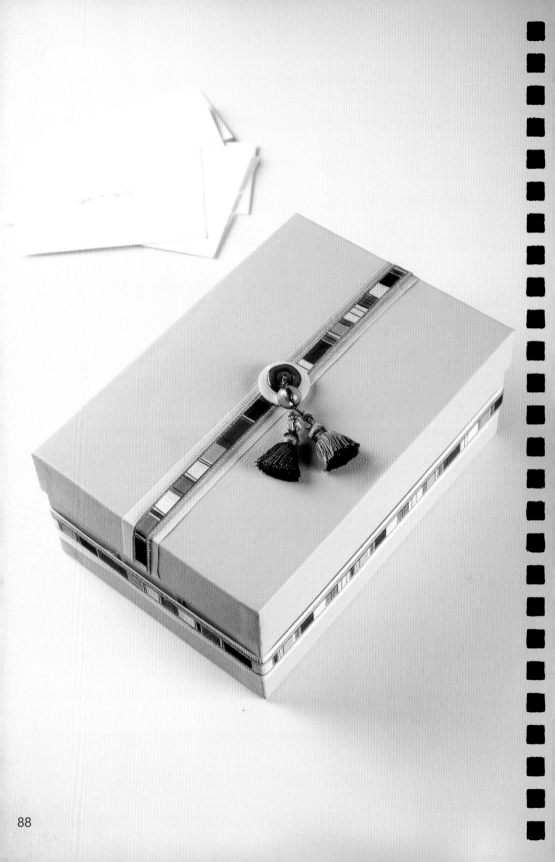

Card Box

Materials

- Acrylic paint: purple
- Adhesives: craft glue, hot glue
- Beaded tassel
- Buttons: coordinating (2)
- Fabric: coordinating
- Foam brush
- Photo storage box
- Ribbon: coordinating (3)
- Scissors: craft, fabric

Instructions

1. Line inside of box with fabric; adhere using craft glue. Trim excess at top and embellish with ribbon.

2. Layer three ribbons and adhere around base of box with craft glue.

3. Paint inside of box top purple; let dry. Layer three ribbons and adhere to box top, securing in place with craft glue.

4. Hot glue buttons together. Cut end of tassel and insert cording through button holes; secure on top of box with hot glue.

time-saving tip

Just as Pretty in Paint

Rather than lining the inside of the photo storage box with fabric, consider spray painting the box a coordinating color.

Photo Stand

Materials

- Adhesives: craft glue, glue stick
- Bone folder
- Brads: small (3)
- Buttons
- Cardstock: heavyweight
- Cosmetic sponge
- Craft scissors
- Decorative paper
- Inkpad: light brown
- Pencil
- Piercing tool
- Ruler
- Wedding photo of guests

Instructions

1. Cut cardstock to 6" x 11". Trace on decorative paper twice; adhere to both sides of cardstock with glue stick.

2. Cut image to 4" x 3½". Adhere to cardstock with glue stick. Add buttons around image with craft glue; let dry completely.

3. Ink edges of photo stand with cosmetic sponge to give aged appearance.

4. Score 1" from shorter edge using bone folder; fold and overlap edges. Create three holes at bottom with piercing tool and insert brads to secure closed.

Sign-In Booklet

Materials

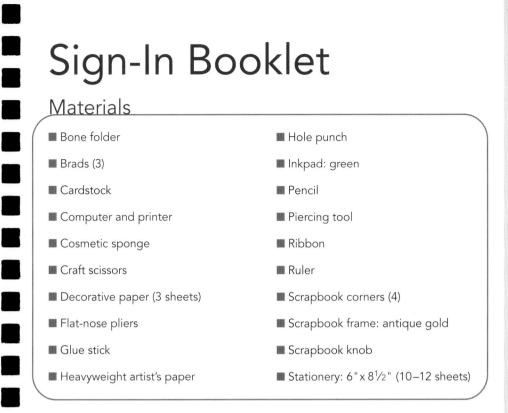

- Bone folder
- Brads (3)
- Cardstock
- Computer and printer
- Cosmetic sponge
- Craft scissors
- Decorative paper (3 sheets)
- Flat-nose pliers
- Glue stick
- Heavyweight artist's paper
- Hole punch
- Inkpad: green
- Pencil
- Piercing tool
- Ribbon
- Ruler
- Scrapbook corners (4)
- Scrapbook frame: antique gold
- Scrapbook knob
- Stationery: 6" x 8½" (10–12 sheets)

Instructions

1. Cut heavyweight paper to 14" x 20" and 1½" x 20".

2. Cut three sheets of decorative paper to 6" x 8½".

3. Score 14" x 20" piece of heavyweight paper down the middle using bone folder; fold over to create "book." Score 1½" x 20" piece of heavyweight paper down the middle using bone folder; fold in half and then insert book. Adhere with glue stick.

4. Stack stationery sheets and punch three evenly spaced holes along left edge, about ¼" in. Using pencil, make three evenly spaced marks where brads will be inserted along spine; make holes using piercing tool and then insert brads. Score front cover along edge of 1½" x 20" strip. *Note:* This will make it easy to keep front cover of book open.

time-saving tip
Color to Coordinate

Rather than spending time looking for embellishments that match in color, simply change the color with a leafing or paint pen.

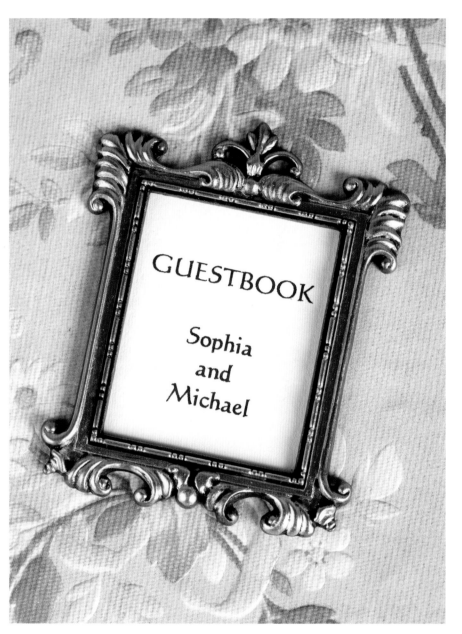

GUESTBOOK

Sophia
and
Michael

Give the Sign-In Booklet cover the attention it deserves with a regal name plate readily available at craft stores.

CHAPTER 6

There are so many beautiful flowers that can be used for wedding celebrations. Just about everything—and everyone—calls for a floral adornment. The great part is that with today's vast array of choices, flowers can be real, silk, dried, or paper. The more the merrier!

Fashion the groom's boutonnière out of dried florals and feathers. Don't forget a blooming halo for the flower girl, and a hand-tied bouquet of calla lilies for the bride.

Centerpieces can be made with a fragrant flower blossom in a glass bowl that's been embellished with ribbon and rhinestones, or create a paper bouquet for a side table. Paper cones can be used to line the pews of an aisle and then transported to the reception and hung from the back of guests' chairs.

Peacock Boutonnière

Materials

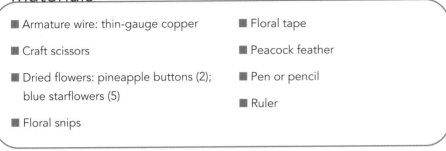

- Armature wire: thin-gauge copper
- Craft scissors
- Dried flowers: pineapple buttons (2); blue starflowers (5)
- Floral snips
- Floral tape
- Peacock feather
- Pen or pencil
- Ruler

Instructions

1. Wrap ends of pineapple button flower stems with floral tape. Add blue starflowers on each side, continuing to wrap with floral tape. Add peacock feather to back, securing with floral tape. *Note:* Floral tape should be wrapped about 1½" down length of stems.

2. Cut wire to 10" length. Starting just below flowers of boutonnière, wrap wire down stem, covering floral tape. Curl 1" ends around pen or pencil to create coils at top and bottom of boutonnière, trimming ends to desired length.

3. Trim ends of dried flowers so they're about ½" below wire using floral snips.

time-saving tip

Alternative Trims

Armature wire lends a modern look to this boutonnière. You could also wrap the flower stems with ribbon or lace, or leave the floral tape exposed.

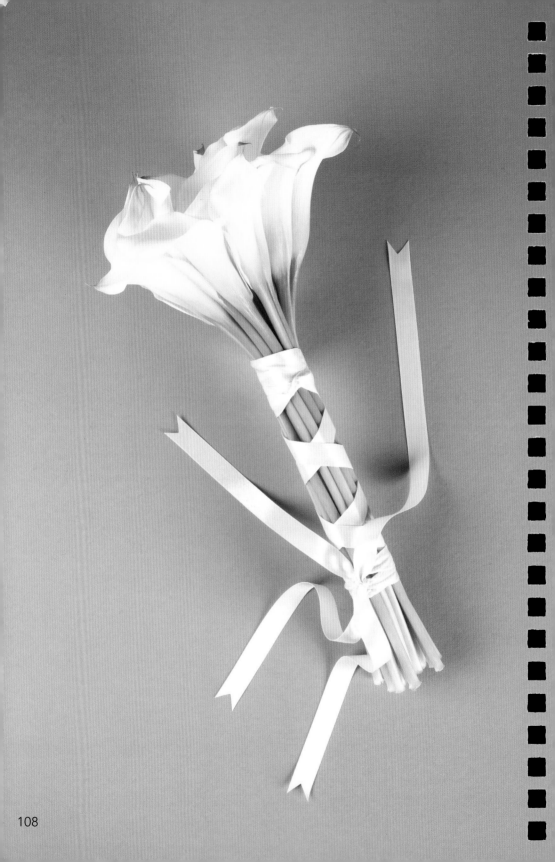

Hand-Tied Bouquet

Materials

- Calla lilies (20)
- Craft scissors
- Floral snips
- Ribbon: satin

Instructions

1. Assemble calla lilies together in an informal gathered style, trimming ends to same length using floral snips.

2. To hand-tie bouquet, wrap a yard of ribbon around the neck of the base of the flowers several times, crossing the free ends of the ribbon and twisting them against themselves each wrap.

3. Tie end of ribbon into knots; trim ribbon ends in inverted "V."

time-saving tip

Handle with Care

Whether you're working with calla lilies or another bouquet of flowers, avoid touching the flower heads; doing so may cause the edges to brown. Also, if you're having a difficult time keeping the layered flowers in place, wrap a twist tie at the top and bottom of the arrangement, hiding the ties with the ribbon.

Paper Flowers

Materials

- Adhesives: floral tape, hot glue
- Cardstock
- Container and filler
- Cotton balls
- Craft scissors
- Floral tape
- Floral wire
- Pencil
- Ribbon: ¼" green; 4" dark green wired
- Ruler

Instructions

1. Trace Petal and Leaf templates (page 112) onto cardstock; cut out. *Note:* You will need about a dozen of the shapes per flower.

2. **To make stamen:** Wrap 4" length of dark green wired ribbon around cotton ball. Insert 15" length of floral wire into cotton ball; wrap wire around base, securing with hot glue. Fold 8" length of dark green ribbon in half, wire to wire; snip ribbon every ⅛", stopping short of wire edge of ribbon. Wrap this ribbon around stamen and hot glue in place. *Note:* The ⅛" widths will naturally form loops.

3. Starting with five small petals, build flower add under stamen; secure using hot glue. Repeat using five large petals. Round edges of petals with pencil to create realistic shape.

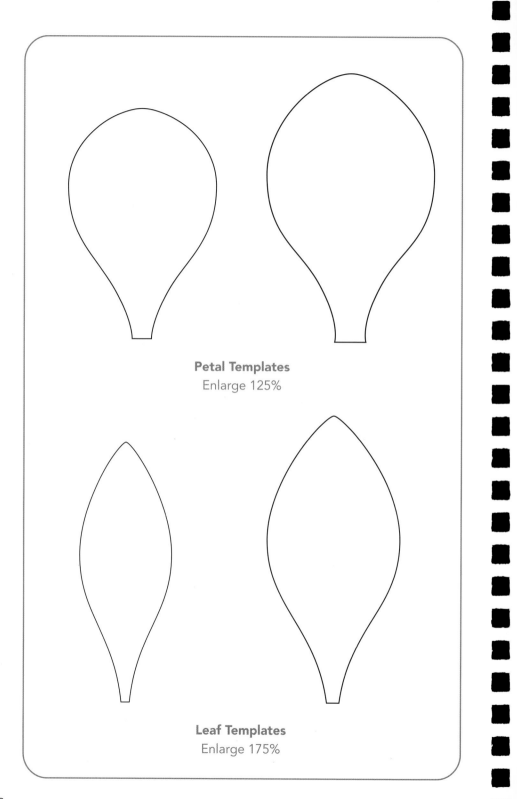

Petal Templates
Enlarge 125%

Leaf Templates
Enlarge 175%

Left: Green moss is an organic filler choice. **Right:** Floral wire adhered to the back of the paper petals allows you to form realistic shapes.

4. Wrap ¼" green ribbon around base of flower; hot glue in place.

5. **To make leaves:** Cut two 12" pieces of floral wire. Hot glue onto back center of two leaves; let dry. Gently bend leaf to create a natural form.

6. Starting at base, wrap floral tape around wire about 3" down stem. Add small leaf, continuing to wrap with floral tape. After another 2", add large leaf, continuing to wrap with floral tape to end of stem; pinch off end of tape.

7. Insert in container and fill with desired materials.

time-saving tip

Add More Color

You may want to consider using two decorative papers for the flower petals. Choose different patterns, like polka dots and stripes, or two different hues; just remember to be sure the colors coordinate.

Floating Orchid

Materials

- Craft glue
- Craft scissors
- Curly willow
- Floral snips

- Glass bowl
- Orchid
- Rhinestones: self-adhesive
- Ribbon

Instructions

1. Wrap ribbon around base of bowl adding $1/4$" for overlap; cut and lay ribbon flat.

2. Add self-adhesive rhinestones every $1/2$", creating desired pattern. Wrap ribbon around bowl, adhering ends with glue.

3. Snip ends of curly willow, about 4", to cut away thicker ends. Wrap curly willow several times, a bit smaller than width of bowl opening; insert in bowl.

4. Fill bowl $2/3$ full with water. Clip end of orchid and float at top of water.

time-saving tip

Rhinestones versus Glitter

If you can't find self-adhesive rhinestones, simply apply craft glue to the back of jewels and adhere to ribbon. Glitter glue dots also create dazzling embellishments, however, they do require more drying time.

Frame Centerpiece

Materials

- Acrylic paint: white
- Cardstock: white
- Craft scissors
- Foam brush
- Glass votive candles (4)
- Hot glue gun and glue sticks
- Ribbon
- Silk flowers (30–40)
- Wire cutters
- Wooden frame

Instructions

1. Paint frame white using foam brush; let dry.

2. Cut cardstock to fit in frame opening; insert.

3. Snip stems off flowers using wire cutters. Adhere to frame with hot glue.

4. Wrap ribbon around perimeter of frame; secure in place with hot glue.

5. Add candles on top of frame opening.

time-saving tip

Getting the Perfect Fit

Instead of four separate votive candles, incorporate a large pillar candle in the center of the frame.

Fresh Flower Arrangement

Materials

- Calla lilies (6–8)
- Floral container
- Floral foam
- Floral snips
- Greenery
- Montecasino asters (4–5 bunches)
- Roses: small red, white (5–7)
- Serrated knife
- Stargazers (3)

Instructions

1. Cut floral foam to fit inside container using serrated knife. Submerge in water, then place in floral container.

2. Starting at the back of the container, add calla lilies in staggered heights. *Note:* Calla lilies should rise about 10"–12" above container.

3. Add row of stargazers and then tuck in roses, Montecasino asters, and greenery at front. Tuck in a few sprigs of Montecasino asters randomly between flowers.

time-saving tip

Any Container Will Do

To preserve your container and extend the life of your flowers, simply insert a piece of water-soaked floral foam in a small zip-top plastic bag. Tuck in flower stems, cinch tight with a rubber band, and insert in container.

Daisy Halo

Materials

- Baby's breath
- Craft scissors
- Daisies (12)
- Floral snips
- Floral tape
- Hot glue gun and glue sticks
- Ribbon
- Ruler
- Wooden halo shape

Instructions

1. Trim daisies so they each have a 2" stem. Lay daisy on outside of halo, wrapping floral tape around base to hold in place. Continue until you have completed a ringlet of daisies.

2. Tuck baby's breath in between daisies, securing on halo with hot glue.

3. Cut two 20" lengths of ribbon. Wrap each length around halo, in between the daisies as show.

4. Tie ends securely, allowing ends to flow freely. Trim ends of ribbon at an angle. Add additional lengths of ribbon, if desired.

time-saving tip

Wire Works Too

If you are unable to locate a wooden halo shape, try using heavy craft wire. Simply shape the wire to fit the flower girl's head and follow the rest of the instructions to add the flowers.

Flower Cone

Materials

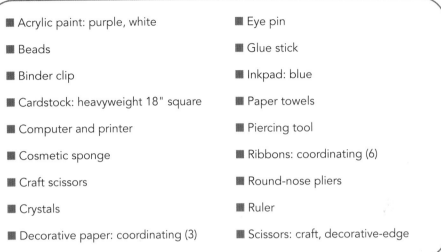

- Acrylic paint: purple, white
- Beads
- Binder clip
- Cardstock: heavyweight 18" square
- Computer and printer
- Cosmetic sponge
- Craft scissors
- Crystals
- Decorative paper: coordinating (3)
- Eye pin
- Glue stick
- Inkpad: blue
- Paper towels
- Piercing tool
- Ribbons: coordinating (6)
- Round-nose pliers
- Ruler
- Scissors: craft, decorative-edge

Instructions

1. Roll heavyweight cardstock into cone shape; secure edges with glue stick and let dry completely. Trim top edge using decorative-edge scissors.

2. Cut or tear 2"–4" wide strips of each piece of decorative paper; adhere to cone with glue stick.

3. Thin white paint with water. Using paper towel, apply light wash over cone. Wipe excess paint with clean paper towel; let dry. Repeat with purple paint. String beads and crystals onto five lengths of various ribbons.

4. Cut 2" off bottom of cone. Apply glue stick inside cone; insert ribbons and close with binder clip about 30 minutes.

5. Layer two ribbons; adhere around top edge of cone with glue stick. Adhere ends of 14" strip of ribbon inside cone to serve as handle. Poke hole in front using piercing tool; string crystal on eye pin and insert into front of cone, securing ends inside cone using pliers. Layer two 4" pieces of ribbons and adhere to bottom of cone.

6. Using computer, print message on cardstock. Cut to 3" x 1", ink edges with cosmetic sponge, and adhere to front of cone with glue stick.

About the Author

Catherine Risling is a talented and experienced journalist who has worked with some of the most dynamic designers in the craft and home décor industries. Rubbing elbows with these talents has nurtured her creative spirit and led her to consult on countless projects, designs, and photo shoots.

Her first book, *Pretty Weddings for Practically Pennies* (©2005 Sterling Publishing, Inc.) included many original and budget-conscious projects she created for her own wedding.

Cathy is the director of editorial for Red Lips 4 Courage Communications, Inc., a book producer for Lark Books and Sterling Publishing, Inc. She has worked for several major metropolitan newspapers and was the executive managing editor of *Romantic Homes* and *Victorian Homes* magazines for several years. Cathy teaches college-level journalism as the newspaper advisor at California State University, Dominguez Hills.

She may have earned her bachelor's degree from California State University, Fullerton, but she credits her travels around the world for inspiring her to see beyond the ordinary. Working behind the scenes, guiding artists and authors in transforming their vision into a book, keeps Cathy happily working in this field.

Cathy lives in Southern California with her husband, Greg, and their adorable yellow lab, Dakota.

Contributors

Lisa Gillis

Lisa has been showing and selling her hand-painted T-shirts, baby clothes, and holiday items at local craft fairs, boutiques, and shows throughout Southern California for several years. She is a decorative faux finish painter and uses her talents for residential and commercial projects alike. After battling and beating breast cancer in 2005, she feels her husband, family, and friends are her greatest inspiration for living life creatively.

Rebecca Ittner

Rebecca spends her days as a freelance photo stylist, editor, and writer based in

Southern California. She has spent the last decade traveling around the country working with artists and authors, helping to bring their dreams to print.

A lifelong love of collecting and crafting continues to bring her joy. Fueled by the genius and inspiration of the women she works with, Rebecca spends any spare time creating—from altered art and books to decoupage and woodworking. Her creations reflect her passions, including family, love, nature, the arts, and travel.

Barbara Schaefer

By day she works in a law office, but at night Barbara Schaefer's creative juices start flowing in her studio. Barbara specializes in painting and jewelling glass and art furniture. Her one-of-a-kind glassware, which is not only beautiful but usable, have been featured in numerous magazines including *Mary Engelbreit's Home Companion* and *Rosie*. Her work can also be seen in the Galerie Michelangelo at Caesars Palace in Las Vegas. Visit www.mykickassglass.com.

METRIC EQUIVALENCY CHARTS

inches to millimeters and centimeters
(mm-millimeters, cm-centimeters)

inches	mm	cm	inches	cm	inches	cm
⅛	3	0.3	9	22.9	30	76.2
¼	6	0.6	10	25.4	31	78.7
½	13	1.3	12	30.5	33	83.8
⅝	16	1.6	13	33.0	34	86.4
¾	19	1.9	14	35.6	35	88.9
⅞	22	2.2	15	38.1	36	91.4
1	25	2.5	16	40.6	37	94.0
1¼	32	3.2	17	43.2	38	96.5
1½	38	3.8	18	45.7	39	99.1
1¾	44	4.4	19	48.3	40	101.6
2	51	5.1	20	50.8	41	104.1
2½	64	6.4	21	53.3	42	106.7
3	76	7.6	22	55.9	43	109.2
3½	89	8.9	23	58.4	44	111.8
4	102	10.2	24	61.0	45	114.3
4½	114	11.4	25	63.5	46	116.8
5	127	12.7	26	66.0	47	119.4
6	152	15.2	27	68.6	48	121.9
7	178	17.8	28	71.1	49	124.5
8	203	20.3	29	73.7	50	127.0

yards to meters

yards	meters	yards	meters	yards	meters	yards	meters	yards	meters
⅛	0.11	2⅛	1.94	4⅛	3.77	6⅛	5.60	8⅛	7.43
¼	0.23	2¼	2.06	4¼	3.89	6¼	5.72	8¼	7.54
⅜	0.34	2⅜	2.17	4⅜	4.00	6⅜	5.83	8⅜	7.66
½	0.46	2½	2.29	4½	4.11	6½	5.94	8½	7.77
⅝	0.57	2⅝	2.40	4⅝	4.23	6⅝	6.06	8⅝	7.89
¾	0.69	2¾	2.51	4¾	4.34	6¾	6.17	8¾	8.00
⅞	0.80	2⅞	2.63	4⅞	4.46	6⅞	6.29	8⅞	8.12
1	0.91	3	2.74	5	4.57	7	6.40	9	8.23
1⅛	1.03	3⅛	2.86	5⅛	4.69	7⅛	6.52	9⅛	8.34
1¼	1.14	3¼	2.97	5¼	4.80	7¼	6.63	9¼	8.46
1⅜	1.26	3⅜	3.09	5⅜	4.91	7⅜	6.74	9⅜	8.57
1½	1.37	3½	3.20	5½	5.03	7½	6.86	9½	8.69
1⅝	1.49	3⅝	3.31	5⅝	5.14	7⅝	6.97	9⅝	8.80
1¾	1.60	3¾	3.43	5¾	5.26	7¾	7.09	9¾	8.92
1⅞	1.71	3⅞	3.54	5⅞	5.37	7⅞	7.20	9⅞	9.03
2	1.83	4	3.66	6	5.49	8	7.32	10	9.14

INDEX